A Pocket Guide to

Confession

A Pocket Guide to
Confession

Michael Dubruiel

Our Sunday Visitor Publishing Division
Our Sunday Visitor, Inc.
Huntington, Indiana 46750

Our Sunday Visitor Publishing Division
Our Sunday Visitor, Inc.
200 Noll Plaza
Huntington, IN 46750

ISBN 978-1-59276-331-3 (Inventory No. T430)
LCCN: 2007932072

Cover design by Amanda Miller
Interior design by Sherri L. Hoffman
Cover photo by W.P. Wittman

PRINTED IN THE UNITED STATES OF AMERICA

"Your sins are forgiven....
Your faith has saved you;
go in peace."
— LUKE 7:48, 50

Contents

Claire Furia Smith, in her book *Catholicism: Now I Get It!*, confessed that when she made her first confession she took a list and a flashlight with her — the list so she wouldn't forget what she had done and the flashlight so she would be able to see the list in the dark confessional. In some ways, Claire's first experience is enlightening: going to confession is all about shedding light on our darkness — letting the light of Christ redefine who God created us to be and letting go of all that tends to define us when we hold on to our list of misdeeds.

"And such were some of you."
If we do not confess our sins, we tend to define ourselves as our sins. We are this or that _____ *(fill in your sinful behavior)*. St. Paul, when reminding the Corinthians about their past lives and the conversion necessary for entrance into the Kingdom of God, says:

*Do you not know that the unrighteous will not inherit the kingdom of God? Do not be deceived; neither the immoral, nor idolaters, nor adulterers, nor homosexuals, nor thieves, nor the greedy, nor drunkards, nor revilers, nor robbers will inherit the kingdom of God. **And such were some of you.** But you were washed, you were sanctified, you were justified in the name of the Lord Jesus Christ and in the Spirit of our God. (1 Corinthians 6:9-11, emphasis added)*

Pope Benedict XVI recently remarked, "How many people also in our time are in search of God, in search of Jesus and of His Church, in search of divine mercy, and are waiting for a 'sign' that will touch their minds and their hearts!"[1]

This pocket guide is meant to serve as an aid to such a varied group as those who:

- Confess regularly
- Are becoming Catholic
- Are making their First Confession

- Have been away from this sacrament for some time
- Are waiting for a "sign" that God can forgive whatever horrible sin has been committed

Each of the above groups of people will obviously use the book differently, but my hope is that all will find it a useful tool.

This great sacrament that Jesus has given to the Church offers each of us the opportunity to once again leave behind whatever the "*such were some of you*" might be in our own lives and reclaim our new identity — not based on our sinfulness, but on the purpose for which God has created us.

Not the "Accuser" but the "Teacher"

It is probable that you are ashamed of your sins. This was the response of our first parents after eating from the forbidden fruit in the Garden of Eden. In the Scriptures, the accusing voice that we hear within is attributed to Satan[2] — in other words its source is evil and keeps us from "coming to our senses" and "returning to the Father."[3] God loves us, became one of us in Jesus, and died for our sins, and He waits in this sacrament to forgive you of your sins so that you may rise to new life in Him.

It is my hope that this book will serve each of you in a way that will help you to experience this sacrament of mercy as one of healing[4] and new life, so that, like St. Mary Magdalene from whom Jesus cast out seven demons, you will, upon hearing Him call your name, say with her, "Teacher."[5]

In this book you will find:

- Answers to basic questions about Confession
- Helps to preparing to make a good Confession by examining your conscience and praying before you celebrate the sacrament
- A walk through the sacrament
- How to use the experience of the Apostle Peter as a model for your own ongoing conversion to Jesus Christ

A Caution

Father Tadeusz Dajczer points out in his excellent book on the spiritual life, *The Gift of Faith*,[6] that there are two ways to experience the sacrament of Reconciliation. The first is an egocentric (meaning a me-centered) way. The second is a theocentric (meaning a God-centered) way. He points out that many times we go to confession in order to feel better about ourselves (an egocentric way) and not out of any real sense that we have hurt God by our actions (a theocentric way).

When I first read Father Dajczer's description of these two ways of celebrating the sacrament, I realized that the hundreds of times (actually perhaps thousands of times) that I have confessed my sins in this sacrament I have done so in the egocentric way — it has been all about me and feeling okay about myself once again.

Our sins rupture our relationship with God. They hurt Him. An analogy might help us understand this better. When a child rejects the love of his or her parents, the parents are hurt by this act. They do not stop loving the child, in fact they suffer all the more because of their love and concern for the child.

Jesus, when He wanted to illustrate God's love and mercy, told just such a story, one that we commonly call the Parable of the Prodigal Son.[7] A boy basically tells his father, "Look, I can't sit around here waiting for you to die, so give me my inheritance now." The father gives it to the child, and the child promptly goes out and squanders it, until he ends up with nothing. Then the child "comes to his senses" and plots a way to return to the father. When the child returns, the father is awaiting him and accepts him readily.

A theocentric celebration of the sacrament will focus more on how my sins hurt God and will be aimed more at my desire to understand the great love that God has for me — manifested by Jesus' death on the Cross — and why my sins are not "the apparent good"[8] that they seem to be when I choose to commit them rather than follow Christ.

This is not only a sacrament of healing, but it is also a sacrament of conversion.[9] When you and I celebrate it with the aim of truly repenting — changing the way we think about the world we live in and viewing it as Christ has taught us and continues to teach us through His Church — then we will be transformed by the Holy Spirit. Our lives will be truly changed. Joy and peace that the world cannot give will be ours. Our hearts and minds will be touched, and our relationship with Christ renewed.[10] This little book is meant to aid you in celebrating the sacrament of Reconciliation in a way that may make that happen in your life.

What are the different names for Confession?

Catholics call the celebration of the Lord's pardon and forgiveness by a variety of names:[11]

- The sacrament of Conversion (*emphasizing our need to return to God*)
- The sacrament of Penance (*expressing the outward sign of our contrition*)
- The sacrament of Confession (*emphasizing the act of naming our sins*)
- The sacrament of Forgiveness (*emphasizing what we receive from God*)
- The sacrament of Reconciliation (*emphasizing the purpose and effect of the sacrament*)

How is the sacrament celebrated?

There are three ways:

- Individually with a priest

- Communally with individual confession to a priest (commonly referred to as a Penance Service)
- Communally with general absolution

How can I celebrate the sacrament individually?

Catholic churches normally have set times when the sacrament is celebrated. If you want to go to confession, you show up at the Church, locate the reconciliation chapel or confessional, and enter when it is available, many times symbolized by a green light or an open door.

You can also call your parish office (or any Catholic Church) to schedule an appointment with a priest to confess. You can also approach a priest and ask him to hear your confession.

How can I celebrate the sacrament communally?

Penance services are often scheduled in parishes during Advent, Lent, parish missions, days of recollection, and retreats. A person can call a parish church to find out when a communal penance service will be held.

How can I celebrate the sacrament with general absolution?

This is a rare occurrence, but it is good to know what the conditions are in case you ever find yourself in such a situation. If someone is in imminent danger of death and there is not time for a priest to hear individual confessions, a priest can grant general absolution to those expressing contrition (sorrow) for their sins. An example of such a situation might be one of the following: soldiers going into battle, passengers aboard an airplane that is about to crash, people living in the path of an approaching deadly storm. Although absolution is given generally (to everyone all at once) in such cases, individuals (who survive) are still required to individually confess their sins to a priest at a later date.

Why can't I just confess my sins to God by myself?

The sacrament of Confession was instituted by the Son of God (Jesus Christ) when He told His disciples: "Receive the Holy Spirit. If you forgive the sins of any, they are forgiven; if you retain the sins of any they are retained."[12] The *Catechism of the Catholic Church* says that Jesus gave this power to forgive sins to the Church by quoting St. Paul: "All this is from God, who through Christ reconciled us to himself and gave us the ministry of reconciliation."[13] God has revealed through Jesus this way of offering His forgiveness to us. How the Church has offered this sacrament has varied over its history (see CCC 1447). We should realize that just as Christ founded the Church and the Church is His Body, we who are in Christ hurt not only God when we sin but the Church. One only has to think of how the sins of Christians damage the visible sign of Christ in the world through His Church.

What steps must one follow in order to celebrate this sacrament fruitfully?

1. Examination of conscience (review one's relationship with God and others)
2. Contrition/repentance (sorrow for one's sins and a desire to not sin again)
3. Confess sins (tell one's sins to a priest)
4. Satisfaction (perform the penance given by the priest)

What are the effects of going to Confession?

The *Compendium of the Catechism of the Catholic Church* lists a number of effects of the sacrament. Confession:

1. Reconciles us with God
2. Forgives our sins
3. Reconciles us with the Church
4. Restores us to the state of grace
5. Remits the eternal punishment merited by our mortal sins
6. Remits, at least in part, the temporal punishment caused by our sins

7. Restores peace
8. Clears our conscience
9. Gives us spiritual consolation
10. Increases our spiritual strength to live the Christian life [14]

Can the priest reveal my sins to another?
No. The sacrament is protected by the Seal of Confession, and anything told to a priest in confession is under that seal. Any priest who breaks this seal would be excommunicated.

What if I feel that I have done something so horrible that God could never forgive me?
Confess it. God's mercy is beyond anything we can do in this lifetime. Do not hold on to your past sins. Bring them to the light of God's mercy in the sacrament and be liberated by His Divine Mercy.

Examining Your Conscience before Confession

The first words that Jesus spoke when He began His public ministry were:

The time is fulfilled, and the kingdom of God is at hand; repent, and believe in the gospel. (Mark 1:15)

Following Christ demands repentance (literally the changing of our minds and hearts). Repentance requires a rethinking of how we view the world — believing in the message that Jesus revealed in the Gospel. Even though we may already be aware of sins that we need to confess, it is wise to once again look at our entire life to see how well we are following Christ. This is called an Examination of Conscience. It is wise to do this as a prayerful way of preparing to celebrate the sacrament.

First, consider this passage from the First Letter of John:

This is the message we have heard from him and proclaim to you, that God is light and in him is no darkness at all. If we say we have fellowship with him while we walk in darkness, we lie and do not live according to the truth; but if we walk in the light, as he is in the light, we have fellowship with one another, and the blood of Jesus his Son cleanses us from all sin. If we say we have no sin, we deceive ourselves, and the truth is not in us. If we confess our sins, he is faithful and just, and will forgive our sins and cleanse us from all unrighteousness. If we say we have not sinned, we make him a liar, and his word is not in us. (1 John 1:5-10)

- Do we walk by the light of Christ and His Gospel?
- Do we trust in Him and the power of this sacrament to truly rid of us of our

sins and give us the grace to begin anew our relationship with Him?

- Do we acknowledge honestly our weaknesses, failings, and sins?

Next, reflect on God's love as spoken of by John:

In this the love of God was made manifest among us, that God sent his only Son into the world, so that we might live through him. In this is love, not that we loved God but that he loved us and sent his Son to be the expiation for our sins. Beloved, if God so loved us, we also ought to love one another. No man has ever seen God; if we love one another, God abides in us and his love is perfected in us. By this we know that we abide in him and he in us, because he has given us of his own Spirit. And we have seen and testify that the Father has sent his Son as the Savior of the world. Whoever confesses that Jesus is the Son of God, God abides in him, and he in God. (1 John 4:9-15)

- Do you love God?
- Do you trust God?
- Do you love everyone?
- Do you believe that Jesus is the Son of God and your Savior?

Observe how St. Paul speaks of those who do not acknowledge God, first in his Letter to the Romans:

And since they did not see fit to acknowledge God, God gave them up to a base mind and to improper conduct. They were filled with all manner of wickedness, evil, covetousness, malice. Full of envy, murder, strife, deceit, malignity, they are gossips, slanderers, haters of God, insolent, haughty, boastful, inventors of evil, disobedient to parents, foolish, faithless, heartless, ruthless. Though they know God's decree that those who do such things deserve to die, they not only do them but approve those who practice them. (Romans 1:28-32)

Then in his Letter to the Colossians:

Put to death therefore what is earthly in you: fornication, impurity, passion, evil desire, and covetousness, which is idolatry. On account of these the wrath of God is coming. In these you once walked, when you lived in them. But now put them all away: anger, wrath, malice, slander, and foul talk from your mouth. Do not lie to one another, seeing that you have put off the old nature with its practices and have put on the new nature, which is being renewed in knowledge after the image of its creator. (Colossians 3:5-10)

In contrast to those who do acknowledge God:

Put on then, as God's chosen ones, holy and beloved, compassion, kindness, lowliness, meekness, and patience, forbearing one another and, if one has a complaint against another, forgiving each other; as the Lord has forgiven you, so you also must forgive.

And over all these put on love, which binds everything together in perfect harmony. And let the peace of Christ rule in your hearts, to which indeed you were called in the one body. And be thankful. Let the word of Christ dwell in you richly, teach and admonish one another in all wisdom, and sing psalms and hymns and spiritual songs with thankfulness in your hearts to God. And whatever you do, in word or deed, do everything in the name of the Lord Jesus, giving thanks to God the Father through him. (Colossians 3:12-17)

- Are your actions more like those of an unbeliever or a believer?
- Do you pray to God at all times? Is God a part of every moment of your life?
- Is there someone or some event that seems more important than God in your life? Have you given power over yourself to something other than God?

A SHORT EXAMINATION OF CONSCIENCE BASED ON THE TEN COMMANDMENTS

The reflections and questions above should help you recommit your life to Christ and His Church. Pages 30-35 contain a modern Examination of Conscience based on the teachings found in the *Catechism of the Catholic Church*.[15]

The Ten Commandments (see Exodus 20:2-17 and Deuteronomy 5:6-21) give us the framework of how we are to love God and our neighbor (Matthew 22:37-40). The worship and love of God comes first and is reflected in the first three commandments. The honor and love of neighbor flows from a right relationship with God — we do not make our parents, country, others and their actions, or material goods a god — thereby we can honor and love all, forgiving their actions when necessary, and using the created goods of the earth rightfully.

1. **I am the LORD your God: you shall not have strange Gods before me.**
   - Do I put my trust in God and not in superstitions or false gods?
   - Do I place my hope in God or do I give in to despair?
   - Do I love God above all created things? Do my actions reflect this love?
   - Do I seek to grow in my relationship with God? Do I pray regularly throughout the day?
   - Do I live my life as though God does not exist?
   - Am I respectful and reverent toward sacred objects?

2. **You shall not take the name of the LORD your God in vain.**
   - Do I praise, honor, and glorify the name of God?
   - Have I used God's name improperly?
   - Have I sworn on God's name and not told the truth?

3. Remember to keep holy the Lord's Day.

- Have I attended Mass faithfully?
- Have I rested, relaxing in mind and body, on the Lord's Day?
- Have I acknowledged in my actions that ultimately everything depends upon God and not on me?

4. Honor your father and your mother.

For a child:
- Do I honor and respect my parents?
- Do I obey them?

For an adult child:
- Have I taken care of my parents if they are infirm or in need?
- Do I honor my parents by accepting their humanity and shortcomings?

For a parent:
- Do I honor and respect my child?
- Do I teach my child the truths of the Catholic Faith?
- Do I teach my child to pray to God and to worship God above all things?

Duties toward civil authority:

- Do I participate and contribute justly to the government of my country?
- Do I put God first and God's law above my country when they are in opposition?

5. You shall not kill.

- Do I respect all human life (from conception to natural death) as sacred and God-given?
- Have I been directly or indirectly involved in an act of abortion, euthanasia, or murder?
- Have I attempted to take my own life or aided someone else to take their life?
- Do I take care of my health and those whom I have responsibility over?
- Do I abuse food, drugs, alcohol, tobacco, or medicine?

6. You shall not commit adultery.

- Do I treat my body as a temple of the Holy Spirit? Do I see others in this way?

- Do I treat my spouse with the dignity of a child of God?
- Am I open in sexual acts with my spouse to sharing in God's creative power?
- Do I view the sexual act as an act of love by giving of myself to my spouse?
- Do I see children as a gift from God?
- Have I committed sexual acts outside of marriage, alone, or with others?
- Have I forced myself sexually upon another person?
- Have I contributed in any way to someone engaged in the sex industry?
- Is my marriage blessed by the Church?

7. You shall not steal.
- Do I respect the goods and property of others?
- Have I taken something that did not rightfully belong to me?
- Have I made restitution?
- Do I honor all contracts that I enter into?
- Do I honor God's creation?

- If I employ someone, do I pay a just wage?
- Do I labor to give my employer the work I am paid for?
- Am I just and fair in all my dealings with others?
- Do I respect the rights of all people as children of the one God?
- Do I share the surplus God has given me with the poor?

8. **You shall not bear false witness against your neighbor.**
   - Do I witness to the truth of the Gospel of Jesus Christ?
   - Have I lied?
   - Have I committed perjury?
   - Have I slandered or defamed another?
   - Have I flattered or praised someone for doing something that was sinful?
   - Have I sought to undo the harm I may have caused by lying about another?

9. You shall not covet your neighbor's wife.

- Am I modest in my dealings with others?
- Do I foster purity in all of my actions?
- Have I dwelt on lustful desires or fueled them by looking at pornography?
- Have I used the Internet as a way of engaging in a sin of lust?
- Have I tempted another to commit a sexual sin?

10. You shall not covet your neighbor's goods.

- Am I thankful for what God has given me?
- Do I experience an inner joy with what I have?
- Do I prefer Christ to everything?
- Do I envy the property of others to the point that I experience sadness?
- Do I spend time lusting after material goods?
- Do I think that riches will make me happy?
- Is my goal in life to do the will of God?

A Prayer to Say before Confessing Your Sins

A Psalm of David, when Nathan the prophet came to him, after he had gone in to Bathsheba.

> Have mercy on me, O God,
> according to your merciful love;
> according to your abundant mercy blot
>   out my transgressions.
> Wash me thoroughly from my iniquity,
> and cleanse me from my sin!
>
> For I know my transgressions,
> and my sin is ever before me.
> Against you, you only, have I sinned,
> and done that which is evil in your sight,
> so that you are justified in your sentence
> and blameless in your judgment.
> Behold, I was brought forth in iniquity,
> and in sin did my mother conceive me.

Behold, you desire truth in the inward
     being;
therefore teach me wisdom in my secret
     heart.
Purge me with hyssop, and I shall be
     clean;
wash me, and I shall be whiter than snow.
Make me hear joy and gladness;
let the bones which you have broken
     rejoice.
Hide your face from my sins,
and blot out all my iniquities.

Create in me a clean heart, O God,
and put a new and right spirit within me.
Cast me not away from your presence,
and take not your holy Spirit from me.
Restore to me the joy of your salvation,
and uphold me with a willing spirit.

Then I will teach transgressors your ways,
and sinners will return to you.
Deliver me from bloodguilt, O God,
O God of my salvation,

and my tongue will sing aloud of your
deliverance.

O Lord, open my lips,
and my mouth shall show forth your
praise.
For you take no delight in sacrifice;
were I to give a burnt offering,
you would not be pleased.
The sacrifice acceptable to God is a
broken spirit;
a broken and contrite heart, O God, you
will not despise.

— PSALM 51:1-17

The Elements of the Sacrament of Penance and Reconciliation (Confession)

On the following pages you will find useful information about the elements that make up the sacrament of Reconciliation and Penance (Confession), including the following:

Help from the Bible — Some of the prayers suggested for Confession are taken from the Bible; so when we use them, we receive help from the Word of God.

Help from the *Compendium* — The *Compendium of the Catechism of the Catholic Church* offers answers to questions we might have; here you will find pertinent questions and answers.

What Does It Mean? — Some of the words that are used in the sacrament are technical. Here we define, in simple English, what they mean.

Posture, Gesture, or What Do I Say? — Often, the most confusing aspect of any sacrament for the uninitiated and even sometimes for lifelong Catholics is what they should be doing with their body at times throughout the sacrament. Here we describe the "how" and the "why."

ENTERING THE CONFESSIONAL OR RECONCILIATION ROOM

The sacrament is most commonly celebrated in a place called a confessional or reconciliation room. However, it may be celebrated anywhere. If you call for an appointment with a priest to make your confession, he may celebrate the sacrament in his office. If you are in the hospital or are homebound, you can ask a priest to celebrate the sacrament there. Most Catholic churches have confessionals or reconciliation rooms where the sacrament is celebrated on a regular basis. There usually is a light or candle that lets one know that the sacrament is being celebrated. These fixed confessionals/reconciliation rooms usually afford the individual the opportunity to make a confession face-to-face or anonymously behind a screen.

If you are celebrating the sacrament in a Catholic church:

- When you enter a Catholic church for the celebration of the sacrament of Reconciliation and Penance (Confession), you first bless yourself with holy water from either a font (small bowl) near the door or the baptismal font located near the entrance of the church.
- Before entering your pew or seat, you genuflect toward the Blessed Sacrament in the tabernacle (look for a lit sanctuary lamp), or if the reservation of the Blessed Sacrament is in a side chapel, bow toward the altar.
- Locate the confessional/reconciliation room. Is there a light or some indication that the sacrament is being offered right now? If there is, there may be a line formed near where the sacrament is being offered.
- Then, kneeling or sitting, you spend some time recollecting yourself in prayer, reviewing in your mind what

you will confess, as well as asking God to reveal any other sins that you should confess today. You may want to offer some prayers of sorrow for your sins to the Lord (you could pray **A Prayer to Say before Confessing Your Sins**, found on page 37).

- After sufficient time, you may want to stand in line (if there is one) or enter the confessional/reconciliation room (if it is open).

POSTURE
Sit or Kneel

If you confess face-to-face, you will take a seat opposite the priest upon entering the reconciliation room. If you go behind the screen anonymously, you will kneel upon entering the confessional.

RECEPTION OF THE PENITENT

What Does It Mean?

You are the penitent, the person who is approaching the sacrament with humble sorrow for your sins. The word penitent is derived from the word repentance, which, of course, is what Jesus preached.

HELP FROM THE BIBLE:

Jesus came into Galilee, preaching the gospel of God, and saying "The time is fulfilled, and the kingdom of God is at hand; *repent*, and believe in the gospel." (Mark 1:15)

The priest will greet you in some fashion. Then you make the sign of the cross, saying the prayer out loud.

GESTURE
Making the Sign of the Cross

Bring the forefingers of your right hand to your forehead while saying, "In the name of the Father," then, tracing downward, touch your chest, "and of the Son," then, tracing toward the left shoulder, "and of the Holy," and then, tracing toward the right shoulder, "Spirit. Amen."

WHAT DO I SAY?

You respond to these words with an "Amen." Amen is a Hebrew word that means "so be it," here meaning that we place ourselves under the Holy Trinity.

HELP FROM THE BIBLE:

"Go therefore and make disciples of all nations, baptizing them *in the name of the Father and of the Son and of the Holy Spirit,* teaching them to observe all that I have commanded you: and behold, I am with you always, to the close of the age." (Matthew 28:19-20)

This Scripture helps us to appreciate that when we make the Sign of the Cross and say this prayer, we call to mind our Baptism, our duties as a follower of Christ, and the assurance of His presence throughout our lives. We identify ourselves as someone who is "in Christ" and in the celebration of this sacrament someone in need of His forgiveness.

The priest will then speak some words of encouragement to you about trusting in God's love and mercy.

HELP FROM THE BIBLE:

"If anyone does sin, we have an advocate with the Father, Jesus Christ the righteous; and he is the expiation of our sins, and not for ours only but also for the sins of the whole world." (1 John 2:1-2)

One of the options the priest may say to you is drawn from this Scripture passage:

> *If you have sinned, do not lose heart.*
> *We have Jesus Christ to plead for us with the Father:*
> *He is the Holy One,*
> *the atonement for our sins*
> *and for the sins of the whole world.*

THE LITURGY OF THE WORD (OPTIONAL)

The priest may read a short passage from Scripture inviting you to listen to what the Lord says to us (this is optional — in my experience, it is rarely used). The passage of Scripture is meant to call to mind both God's mercy and our call to conversion.

HELP FROM THE BIBLE:

"But God shows his love for us in that while we were yet sinners Christ died for us. Since, therefore, we are now justified by his blood, much more shall we be saved by him from the wrath of God." (Romans 5:8-9)

This is one possible reading the priest might use.

CONFESSION AND PENANCE

We then confess our sins.

WHAT DO I SAY?

You may use whatever words you would like, but it is helpful to use the following formula as a way of staying focused:

> Bless me father, for I have sinned. It has been (number of weeks, months, or years) since my last confession (or "This is my first confession"). These are my sins.

You then list your sins, telling him what you have done and how often you have done it (if more than once).

The priest will help you if you have trouble. He may ask questions if he is unsure of what you mean. Answer honestly. Trust in

God's love and mercy, let go of your sins in this moment of grace.

HELP FROM THE *COMPENDIUM*:

Which sins must be confessed?[16]

All grave sins not yet confessed, which a careful examination of conscience brings to mind, must be brought to the sacrament of Penance. The confession of serious sins is the only ordinary way to obtain forgiveness.

The priest will then impose a penance. He may ask you to say certain prayers or to do a charitable work. If for some reason, you feel you cannot do it — for instance, you don't know the prayer he asks you to do as a penance — you should tell him. He may modify the penance or tell you where you can find the prayer. Your fulfillment of the penance is called making satisfaction and it is an important element of the sacrament.

What Does It Mean?

Penance is an act performed to show sorrow for sin. There are two types of penance: interior penance (our inner being striving toward God and away from sin) and exterior acts of penance (prayer, fasting, and giving to the poor) that help us to move out of ourselves and toward God.

Some sample penances include but certainly are not limited to:

- Say three Our Fathers
- Perform an act of kindness
- Say a prayer for the person you have hurt

ACT OF CONTRITION

The priest then asks you to say an Act of Contrition or to express your sorrow.

WHAT DO I SAY?

You are free to express your sorrow in whatever words you would like. You may use a simple prayer such as, **"Lord Jesus Christ, Son of God, have mercy on me, a sinner"** *(the Jesus Prayer), or you may use one of these forms of the Act of Contrition:*

Act of Contrition (Traditional)

O my God, I am heartily sorry for having offended Thee, and I detest all my sins because of thy just punishments, but most of all because they offend Thee, my God, who art all good and deserving of all my love. I firmly resolve with the help of Thy grace to sin no more and to avoid the near occasion of sin. Amen.[17]

Act of Contrition (Modern)

My God,
I am sorry for my sins with all my heart.
In choosing to do wrong
and in failing to do good,
I have sinned against You
whom I should love above all things.
I firmly intend, with Your help,
to do penance,
to sin no more,
and to avoid whatever leads me to sin.
Our Savior Jesus Christ
suffered and died for us.
In His name, my God, have mercy.

The modern version of the Act of Contrition is printed on the back cover of this book in case you want to take it with you.

Regardless of what words you choose to express your sorrow to God, what matters is that you do it in a heartfelt manner.

ABSOLUTION

The priest will then extend his hands over your head (if you are celebrating the sacrament face-to-face) or extend his right hand toward the confessional screen (if you are celebrating the sacrament in that fashion), as he says the words of absolution:

> God, the Father of mercies, through the death and the resurrection of His Son has reconciled the world to himself and sent the Holy Spirit among us for the forgiveness of sins; through the ministry of the Church may God give you pardon and peace, and I absolve you from your sins in the name of the Father, and of the Son, and of the Holy Spirit.

WHAT DO I SAY?

When he concludes the prayer, you say: "Amen."

DISMISSAL

After the prayer of absolution, the priest will dismiss you. Again, there are a number of options for the priest to use. Here are a few of the more common ones:

- *The priest says,* "Give thanks to the Lord, for He is good."
  You say, "His mercy endures for ever."

- *The priest says,* "The Lord has freed you from your sins. Go in peace."
  (There is no standard response for the penitent to say.)

- *The priest says,* "May the Passion of our Lord Jesus Christ, the intercession of the Blessed Virgin Mary, and of all the saints, whatever good you do and suffering you endure, heal your sins, help you to grow in holiness, and reward you with eternal life. Go in peace."
  (There is no standard response for the penitent to say.)

Once the priest has dismissed you, you rise and leave the reconciliation room/confessional. You may wish to recite a prayer of thanksgiving to God (you may use one of the **Prayers to Say After Confession** found on pages 59-64).

Prayers to Say after Confession (Along with Your Penance)

A Psalm of Thanksgiving

I love the LORD, because he has heard
my voice and my supplications.
Because he inclined his ear to me,
therefore I will call on him as long
    as I live.
The snares of death encompassed me;
the pangs of Sheol laid hold on me;
I suffered distress and anguish.
Then I called on the name of the LORD:
"O LORD, I beg you, save my life!"

Gracious is the LORD, and righteous;
our God is merciful.
The LORD preserves the simple;
when I was brought low, he saved me.
Return, O my soul, to your rest;

for the LORD has dealt bountifully
    with you.

For you have delivered my soul
    from death,
my eyes from tears,
my feet from stumbling;
I walk before the LORD
in the land of the living.

I kept my faith, even when I said,
"I am greatly afflicted";
I said in my consternation,
"Men are all a vain hope."

What shall I render to the LORD
for all his bounty to me?
I will lift up the chalice of salvation
and call on the name of the LORD,
I will pay my vows to the LORD
in the presence of all his people.
Precious in the sight of the LORD
is the death of his saints.
O LORD, I am thy servant;

I am thy servant, the son of thy
   handmaid.
You have loosed my bonds.
I will offer to you the sacrifice of
   thanksgiving
and call on the name of the LORD.
I will pay my vows to the LORD
in the presence of all his people,
in the courts of the house of the LORD,
in your midst, O Jerusalem.
Praise the LORD!

— PSALM 116

A Prayer of Firm Purpose
of Following Christ

O Lord, I place myself in your hands and
dedicate myself to you. I pledge myself to do
your will in all things: To love you with all
my heart, all my soul, all my strength. Not to
kill. Not to steal. Not to covet. Not to bear
false witness. To honor all persons. Not to do
to another what I would not wish done to
myself.

Not to seek after pleasures. To love fasting. To relieve the poor. To clothe the naked. To visit the sick. To bury the dead. To help in trouble. To console the sorrowing. To hold myself aloof from worldly ways. To prefer nothing to the love of Christ. Not to give way to anger. Not to foster a desire for revenge. Not to entertain deceit in the heart. Not to make a false peace. Not to forsake charity.

To speak the truth with heart and tongue. Not to return evil for evil. To do no injury: even to bear patiently any injury done to me. To love my enemies. Not to curse those who curse me, but rather to bless them. To bear persecution for justice' sake. Not to be proud. Not to be given to intoxicating drink. Not to be an over-eater. Not to be lazy. Not to be slothful. Not to be a complainer. Not to be a gossip. To put my trust in you. To refer the good I see in myself to you. To refer any evil in myself to myself. To fear the day of judgment. To be in dread of hell. To desire eternal life with spiritual longing. To keep death before my eyes daily. To keep constant watch over my actions.

To remember that you see me everywhere. To call upon Christ for defense against evil thoughts that arise in my heart. To guard my tongue against wicked speech. To avoid much speaking. To avoid idle talk. To read only what is good to read. To look at only what is good to see. To pray often. To ask forgiveness daily for my sins, and to seek ways to amend my life.

Not to desire to be thought holy, but to seek holiness. To fulfill your commandments by good works. To love chastity. To hate no one. Not to be jealous or envious of anyone. Not to love strife. Not to love pride. To honor the aged. To pray for my enemies. To make peace after a quarrel, before the setting of the sun. Never to despair of your mercy, O God of Mercy.

Amen.

— ST. BENEDICT OF NURSIA

A Prayer for the Intercession of Mary, Mother of Mercy

O Lady and Mother of mercy who gave the world the Savior, consent to be my intercessor. I flee to your most gracious and singular protection, and ask you, O most faithful one, to incline the ears of your faithfulness to my prayers. I strongly fear that my life may not be pleasing to your Son, and I entreat Him that, just as He manifested himself to the world through you, so too, I beg, may He have pity on me without delay for your sake.

Amen.

— St. Odo of Cluny

Meditation: Making Confession a Life-Changing Experience

Simon and his coworkers had been fishing all night long without any luck. Despite their hard work, when morning came they had nothing to show for their efforts.

While they were cleaning their nets near the shore, a stranger approached and asked to use one of their boats. Jesus of Nazareth instructed them to pull out a bit from the shore, and then He sat and preached to a crowd gathered on the shore from the boat anchored in shallow water.

When Jesus had finished speaking to the crowds, He turned and spoke to Simon, "Put out into the deep and let down your nets for a catch" (Luke 5:4).

Simon was tired and really didn't feel like fishing anymore, but Jesus' preaching had moved him, so he said, "At your word I will let down the nets" (Luke 5:5).

Then something happened. When Simon did what Jesus told him to do, he caught so many fish that his boat nearly sank from the weight of the fish gathered.

The Gospel of Luke records Simon's reaction:

But when Simon Peter saw it, he fell down at Jesus' knees, saying "Depart from me, for I am a sinful man, O Lord." For he was astonished. (Luke 5:8-9)

"Astonished" doesn't quite get it. The Greek word that Luke uses has the sense that Simon was literally "frightened." Considering how he must have wondered at that moment what type of man Jesus was, this is totally understandable.

Simon Peter had been working all night, doing what he did for a living, with very little success. Now suddenly, after following Jesus' instructions, he gets this amazing result. Most of us would like to experience the power of Jesus in our lives, but perhaps have fallen into a lethargy — when it comes to our sins, we feel like we've been working at it all our lives with little improvement. In this Gospel story about Simon Peter, we can find help in transforming our experience of the sacrament of Penance and Reconciliation. Here is the passage:

While the people pressed upon [Jesus] to hear the word of God, he was standing by the lake of Gennesaret. And he saw two boats by the lake; but the fishermen had gone out of them and were washing their nets. Getting into one of the boats, which was Simon's, he asked him to put out a little from the land. And he sat down and taught the people from the boat. And when he had ceased speaking, he said to Simon, "Put out into the deep and let down your nets for a catch." And Simon answered, "Master, we toiled all night and took nothing! But at your word I will let down the nets." And when they had done this, they enclosed a great shoal of fish; and as their nets were breaking, they beckoned to their partners in the other boat to come and help them. And they came and filled both the boats, so that they began to sink. But when Simon Peter saw it, he fell down at Jesus' knees, saying, "Depart from me, for I am a sinful man, O Lord." For he was astonished, and all that were with him, at the catch of fish which they had taken; and so also were James and John, sons of Zebedee, who were partners with Simon. And Jesus said to Simon, "Do not be afraid; henceforth you will be catching men." And when they had brought their boats to land, they left everything and followed him. (Luke 5:1-11)

Try the following steps, drawn from the Gospel.

1. Acknowledge your failure.

The first step to truly being open to the power of Christ in your life is to admit your own inability to save yourself. This is a hard lesson. Often when we come to celebrate the sacrament of Confession, we acknowledge that we have failed, but we fail to acknowledge that we

HELP FROM THE BIBLE:

"Two men went up into the temple to pray, one a Pharisee and the other a tax collector. The Pharisee stood and prayed thus with himself, 'God, I thank thee that I am not like other men, extortioners, unjust, adulterers, or even like this tax collector. I fast twice a week, I give tithes of all that I get.' But the tax collector, standing far off, would not even lift up his eyes to heaven, but beat his breast, saying, 'God, be merciful to me a sinner!' I tell you, this man went down to his house justified rather than the other; for every one who exalts himself will be humbled, but he who humbles himself will be exalted." (Luke 18:10-14)

Jesus gives us an example of humble prayer — a prayer that God hears and rewards. Is my prayer like that of the Pharisee or the tax collector?

have found ourselves helpless, powerless to do better.

The apostles were fisherman, they had fished all night, but they had caught nothing. They couldn't do it on their own — they even seemed reluctant to try what Jesus suggested, but they tried it anyway.

Follow their example. You've tried to avoid the near occasion of sin, and you've failed. You've tried not to fall into the same sins, but you've failed. You've worked hard at it, but you haven't been able to save yourself. Admit that you are likely to fail again if it is left up to you. Leave the confessional with this in your mind: "I'm likely to commit this sin again if I do not totally rely on God."[18] Then entrust yourself to Jesus.

2. Make it personal.

Too often, we approach God in an abstract way. Jesus has given a human face to God. Get to know Him:

- Read about Him in the Bible.
- Pray the Rosary and Meditate on the Mysteries of His Life.
- Practice devotion to Him.

The real Jesus that we encounter in the Bible hardly ever matches up to what we are apt to think He is like. We will encounter someone who will challenge the way we think about life and how we are to live. We will also encounter in Jesus the love that God has for us. God's love is not abstract as we often make it out to be when we do not think about Jesus. God's love for you is revealed in Jesus, and there is great power in that love and forgiveness!

Let the love of Christ empower you to "put out into the deep," to experience His grace that you receive in the sacrament of Penance and Reconciliation. When you find yourself tempted, admit your powerlessness — go ahead and tell Jesus that you've been working on this sin all of your life and haven't had any success (sort of like fishing all night and catching nothing), admit that you need His help, and wait for a miraculous result!

When it comes to your relationship with Christ, always approach Him as a beggar — we desperately need what He can give us! See your failure as hurting your relationship with Jesus, a relationship that your very life depends on.

HELP FROM THE BIBLE:

The neighbors and those who had seen him before as a beggar, said, "Is not this the man who used to sit and beg?" Some said, "It is he"; others said, "No, but he is like him." He said, "I am the man." They said to him, "Then how were your eyes opened?" He answered, "The man called Jesus made clay and anointed my eyes and said to me, 'Go to Siloam and wash'; so I went and washed and received my sight." (John 9:8-11)

3. Expect to be tempted.

Life is full of temptations, and there is a glamour of evil that we have to be real about. Forbidden fruit looks good. When Eve was tempted in the Garden of Eden by the serpent, she saw:

- "That the tree was good for food" (Genesis 3:6)
- "That it was a delight to the eyes" (Genesis 3:6)
- "That the tree was desired to make one wise" (Genesis 3:6)

Only then did she take and eat of the deadly fruit!

So it is with almost anything sinful. We have to realize and believe that God knows more than we do. We have to trust God even when it seems to us that this sin isn't going to harm ourselves or anyone. We have to imitate Christ and embrace the Cross by again turning to Him and admitting our own powerlessness, sometimes even crying out in our lack of faith, "Save us, Lord; we are perishing" (Matthew 8:25).

Each Easter when we renew the promises we made at our Baptism, we are asked whether we reject Satan. One variation of the renewal asks us, "Do you reject the glamour of evil, and refuse to be mastered by sin?"

Know that in temptation evil can appear glamorous and that we can often feel that we are mastered by our sins — but all of this is an opportunity to cry out to God who can save us!

4. Make God the center of your life.

St. Paul instructs us to pray always. How much time do you spend talking to God every day?

Even though you may have only a certain amount of time to spend in formal prayer every day, there is nothing stopping you from making every moment of your life a dialogue with God.

The apostles had left everything to follow Jesus, but Jesus still accused them of having little faith, because even though they walked behind Jesus, they did not see the world they lived in with the eyes of faith.

Jesus lived in the real world. Too often we live in a fantasy world and are unhappy because the world isn't the way we would like it. Living in faith means seeing the world as Jesus sees it, asking: "Why has God put me here?" "Why is God sending this person to me?" We shoul see even the temptations we face as reminders to turn back to God who alone can give us joy and life, as Pope Benedict XVI has said: "It is good to recognize one's weakness because that way we know that we need the grace of God."[19]

Invite God into every moment of your life. Beg His help, grace, and love in all things. Have faith and trust in Him, and He will give you pardon and lasting peace.

HELP FROM THE BIBLE:

"Therefore I tell you, do not be anxious about your life, what you shall eat or what you shall drink, nor about your body, what you shall put on. Is not life more than food, and the body more than clothing? Look at the birds of the air: they neither sow nor reap nor gather into barns, and yet your heavenly Father feeds them. Are you not of more value than they? And which of you by being anxious can add one cubit to his span of life?

"And why are you anxious about clothing? Consider the lilies of the field, how they grow; they neither toil nor spin; yet I tell you, even Solomon in all his glory was not arrayed like one of these. But if God so clothes the grass of the field, which today is alive and tomorrow is thrown into the oven, will he not much more clothe you, O men of little faith? Therefore do not be anxious, saying, 'What shall we eat?' or 'What shall we drink?' or 'What shall we wear?' For the Gentiles seek all these things; and your heavenly Father knows that you need them all. But seek first his kingdom and his righteousness, and all these things shall be yours as well." (Matthew 6:25-33)

Notes

[1] Homily of His Holiness Benedict XVI, Fourth Sunday of Lent, March 26, 2006.

[2] The literal meaning of Satan is "adversary" or "accuser."

[3] See the Parable of the Prodigal Son (Luke 15:11-32).

[4] The *Catechism of the Catholic Church* places the sacrament of Reconciliation and Penance (Confession) along with the Anointing of the Sick as a sacrament of Healing (cf. CCC 1420ff). The example of the healing of the paralytic (cf. Mark 2-12) is given as an example of someone Jesus heals both of a physical malady and of sinfulness.

[5] "Jesus said to her, 'Mary.' She turned and said to him in Hebrew, 'Rab-boni!' (which means Teacher)" (John 20:16).

[6] Tadeusz Dajczer, *The Gift of Faith*. Ventura, CA: In the Arms of Mary Foundation, 2001, pp. 85-89.

[7] Pope Benedict XVI in his book *Jesus of Nazareth* gives an excellent commentary on this parable (pp. 202ff).

[8] Genesis 3:6.

[9] CCC 1423.

[10] Pope Benedict XVI, in *Jesus of Nazareth* (p. xii), points out that "intimate friendship with Christ" is something upon "which everything depends."

[11] CCC 1423-1442.

[12] John 20:22-23.

[13] CCC 1442, 2 Corinthians 5:18.

[14] *Compendium of the Catechism of the Catholic Church* 310

[15] CCC 2083ff.

[16] *Compendium of the Catechism of the Catholic Church* 304 (cf. CCC 1456).

[17] *Compendium of the Catechism of the Catholic Church*, Appendix A, Common Prayers. Though there are a variety of forms of the Act of Contrition, this standard form appears in the *Catechism*.

[18] I picked this idea up from a book written in the 1940s by Fr. Alfred Wilson entitled *Pardon and Peace*. In that book, Fr. Wilson counseled the reader to think, "I probably will commit this sin again." I think my rendering captures what Fr. Wilson meant by this counsel.

[19] Address to Seminarians, February 17, 2007.